How
Many
Ways...

Steve Jenkins &
Robin Page

Houghton Mifflin Company • Boston 2008

...Can You Catch A Fly?

All animals must find or catch food to stay alive. Most have to avoid being eaten themselves. Others may need to make shelters or build nests. And some are trying to hatch their eggs and protect their young. There are millions of different kinds of animals, and they have come up with some ingenious solutions to these problems. See if you can figure out how the animals in these pages will snare a fish, hatch an egg, use a leaf, catch a fly, dig a hole, or eat a clam. If you'd like more information about these animals, you can find it at the back of the book.

How many ways can you snare a fish?

Fish are slippery, quick, and good at escaping danger. But they have clever enemies, and most face the constant threat of being eaten by other animals.

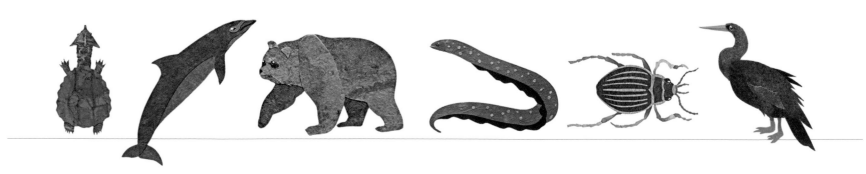

A **diving beetle** can breathe underwater from a bubble of air trapped beneath its wings. It seizes a fish with its legs and devours it with powerful jaws.

The **anhinga** (an-*hing*-guh) dives underwater for fish or stalks them in the shallows. It stabs a fish with its sharp bill, tosses it into the air, and swallows it headfirst.

As salmon swim upstream to lay their eggs, a **grizzly bear** waits. It stands in the rapids and grabs fish in midair as they leap from the water.

As a group of **dolphins** circles beneath a school of fish, each dolphin blows a stream of bubbles. The fish crowd together inside this bubble "net," and the dolphins swim straight up through the fish, snapping them up left and right.

The **electric eel** uses special organs along its body to produce a powerful jolt of electricity that can stun or kill its prey.

The **matamata** (*ma*-ta-*ma*-ta) rests on the bottom of a lake or stream. When a fish comes near, it sticks out its neck, opens its mouth, and expands its throat. The sudden suction pulls the fish into the turtle's mouth.

How many ways can you hatch an egg?

Many animals reproduce by laying eggs. Some try to guarantee that they will have surviving offspring by laying thousands — even millions — of eggs. Most of the eggs won't make it, but chances are at least a few will hatch. Other animals produce only a few eggs but take better care of them, sometimes in surprising ways.

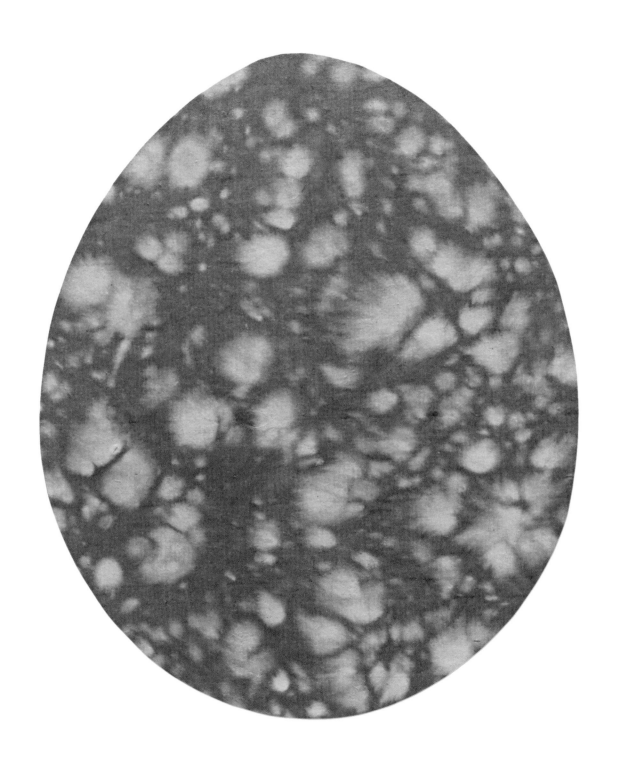

Earwigs are among the few insects that take care of their eggs. A mother earwig curls her body around her eggs to keep them safe and constantly licks them to keep them moist and clean.

The **white tern** lives on islands with few predators, so it doesn't bother to make a nest.

It lays its single egg in the open, often balanced on a tree branch.

After a mother **Surinam toad** (*soor*-uh-nahm) lays her eggs, the father places them on the skin of her back. There, in small pits, tadpoles hatch from the eggs. After a few months, the tadpoles have become little toads, and they push their way out.

Almost all mammals give birth to live young. The **echidna** (ih-*kid*-nuh) is an exception — the mother lays eggs, placing them in a pouch on her belly.

Young echidnas, known as puggles, spend several weeks in the pouch after hatching.

The **ichneumon wasp** (ik-*noo*-muhn) lays its eggs inside a caterpillar. When the eggs hatch, the wasp larvae eat the caterpillar from the inside out.

A mother **Polynesian megapode** buries her eggs in ash at the rim of a volcanic crater. The heat of the volcano keeps them warm until they hatch.

How many ways can you use a leaf?

Leafy green plants cover much of the earth. Leaves are important to both plants and animals, because they can make food from sunlight, air, and water. Many animals eat leaves, but some creatures have found more unusual uses for them.

Using her sharp beak and silk from a spider's web, a **tailorbird** sews a leaf into a pouch that will hold her nest and eggs.

Leaf-cutting ants snip leaves into pieces and carry them to their nest. There the leaves are used to grow a fungus that is "farmed" in underground chambers. This fungus becomes food for the ants.

The **orangutan** (aw-*rang*-oo-tan) lives in the rainforest. To stay dry, it sometimes uses a large leaf as an umbrella.

Capuchin monkeys (cap-*yoo*-chin) rub their bodies with the leaves of certain trees. They probably do this to keep insects away as well as to make themselves smell good to other monkeys.

When **white tent bats** need a place to sleep, they bite through the ribs of a leaf in several places. The sides of the leaf droop down, turning it into a "tent."

Stepping from one lily pad to another, the **lily trotter** can walk over the surface of a pond without even getting its toes wet.

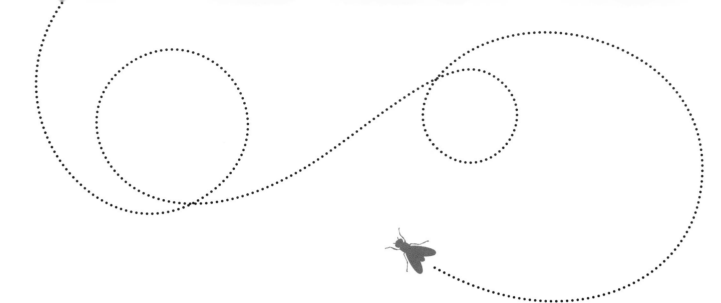

How many ways can you catch a fly?

Flies are *fast*. They can hover, fly backwards, and walk upside down. Their large eyes watch for danger, and their lightning-fast reflexes help them escape it. Flies are found almost everywhere on earth, but to catch one you've got to be very quick, very tricky, or both.

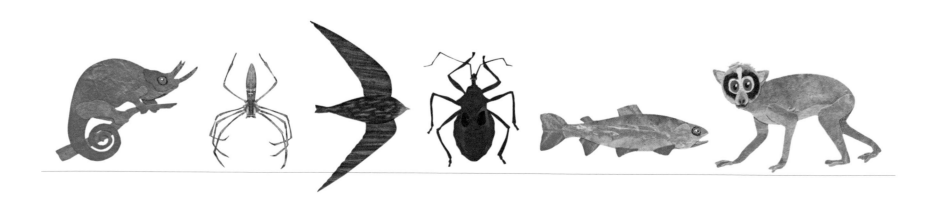

A **rainbow trout** leaps completely out of the water to snatch a fly that ventures close to the surface.

The **net-casting spider** weaves a square web, which it holds by the corners as it waits, hanging upside down. When a fly walks below, the spider stretches the web "net" wide and pushes it down over its victim.

The **Jackson's chameleon** has a sticky tongue one and a half

The acrobatic **chimney swift** uses its aerial skills to catch and eat thousands of flies and other airborne insects a day. This bird spends nearly its entire life in the air, eating, drinking, and even sleeping in flight.

This **assassin bug** stalks its prey and spears it with a swift stab of its poisonous swordlike "beak."

A **slender loris** moves carefully through the trees. It approaches its prey stealthily and extends its long, thin arms. When it's close enough, the loris lunges and grabs the fly with both hands.

times the length of its body. It can snap up a fly in less time than it takes you to blink.

How many ways can you dig a hole?

Animals dig into mud, dirt, and rock to make homes, escape from enemies, or find food. They've evolved many different ways of making holes, often using body parts that are specially adapted for digging.

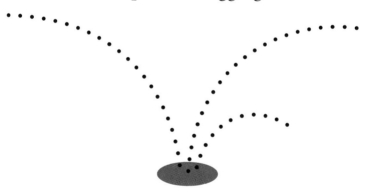

The **worm lizard** looks like a large earthworm, but it is actually a lizard without legs. This reptile makes tunnels by driving its wedge-shaped head into the earth.

The **red rock urchin** wears away the rock or coral of the sea floor with its teeth. Occasionally, a sea urchin grows too large to get out of the hole it has made, and it must remain there for the rest of its life.

The **burrowing parrot** uses its beak to dig nesting holes in cliffs of solid rock.

The **prairie mole cricket** has front legs shaped like shovels. With them, it digs a Y-shaped burrow that acts as a loudspeaker, amplifying the cricket's mating call.

The **Mexican burrowing toad** digs into the mud with its large back feet, moving in a spiral as it burrows. The toad sucks in air as it digs, inflating its body like a balloon and pushing out the mud walls of its hole.

The **aardvark** may be the fastest digger in the animal world. It uses its strong front legs and long claws to make underground burrows, sometimes excavating a new hole each night.

How many ways can you eat a clam ?

A clam holds the two halves of its shell together with powerful muscles. The shell itself is tough and hard. Additionally, most clams live buried in sand or mud and aren't easy to spot. Many animals like to eat clams, however, and they've devised ingenious ways of finding them and getting to the soft creature inside.

The club-shaped foot of the **mantis shrimp** delivers a kick with such force that it can shatter a clam's shell. The same kick can break the glass wall of an aquarium.

The **whelk** uses a special tube to drill a hole through the clam's shell, killing it. The whelk then sucks the clam's body from its shell.

With its long fingers and sharp claws, a **raccoon** pries open a clam's shell.

A **herring gull** picks up a clam and carries it high into the air. It drops the clam repeatedly on rocks or pavement until the shell shatters.

The **bat ray** uses its wings to fan away the sand and mud of the sea floor. When it uncovers a clam, the ray crushes its shell with powerful jaws and spits out the pieces.

A **sea star** wraps its arms around a clam. With hundreds of tiny suction cups, it pulls until the clam is exhausted and opens its shell. Next, the sea star pushes its own stomach out through its mouth right into the clam's shell and digests the clam in place.

How many ways can you . . .

. . . snare a fish?

There are thousands of different kinds, or species, of **diving beetles.** They live in streams and ponds in most parts of the world, and can be as much as two inches (5 centimeters) in length. The diving beetle is a fierce hunter. It lies motionless in the water until an insect, tadpole, or fish comes close. Then, with a sudden lunge, the beetle grabs its prey with strong legs and sharp jaws. Diving beetles leave the water and fly around at night, and a person who picks one up can get a sharp pinch.

Grizzly bears live in the mountains of the northwest United States and western Canada. A male grizzly can weigh as much 1,500 pounds (680 kilograms) and stand nearly ten feet (3 meters) tall. Grizzlies are omnivores — they eat roots, nuts, berries, insects, fish, and mammals. These huge bears may look lumbering and slow, but they can easily outrun a human.

The **matamata** (*ma*-ta-*ma*-ta) is a large turtle, with a shell up to 16 inches (41 centimeters) long. It lives in South American rivers and lakes. Algae and mud coat the turtle's rough shell, giving it the appearance of a pile of rocks as it sits quietly on the bottom. If a fish, frog, or small mammal gets close, the matamata sucks it in and swallows it whole.

The **anhinga** (an-*hing*-guh), or snakebird, lives near lakes and marshes in the southeastern United States and South America. This bird has a body about 32 inches (81 centimeters) in length. Together, its neck and bill are as long as its body. The anhinga searches for fish as it swims, often diving to chase its prey underwater.

Like whales, **dolphins** are mammals and have to come to the surface to breathe. The dolphin in this book is a bottlenose, found in all the warm oceans of the world. Bottlenose dolphins reach 12 feet (3 ½ meters) in length. They are intelligent animals that can communicate with each other by making a variety of squeaks, clicks, and whistles. Dolphins form groups to herd and catch fish and squid, which they swallow whole.

The **electric eel** is actually a kind of knifefish. It lives in the tropical rivers of South America and grows to eight feet (2 ½ meters) in length. Using special electricity-producing organs, the eel can produce discharges of 600 volts. A shock this strong

. . . hatch an egg?

can stun an animal as large as a horse, and it easily kills the fish and small mammals the eel feeds on. A weak electric field around the eel's body allows it to detect fish in murky water.

The **Surinam toad** (*soor*-uh-nahm), also known as the star-fingered toad, is about seven inches (18 centimeters) long. It lives in lakes and streams in the rainforests of South America and eats fish, which it locates with its long, sensitive fingers. The female lays as many as 100 eggs, which the male arranges on the skin of her back. The skin swells around them, creating a little pit for each egg. After the eggs hatch, the tadpoles remain in pockets on the mother's back for a few months. When the little toads are fully formed, they push their way out and swim away.

There are close to 2,000 species of earwig, found almost everywhere on earth. These insects like damp, dark places, including the basements and bathrooms of people's homes. Earwigs got their name from an old belief that they crawl into humans' ears, burrow into their brains, and lay their eggs. It is possible that at times earwigs have crawled into people's ears, which are dark and moist, but they do not lay eggs there, and they certainly don't burrow into anyone's brain. Earwigs are about a half-inch (12 millimeters) long. They eat other insects, plants, and garbage.

Ichneumon wasps (ik-*noo*-muhn) are found in temperate climates worldwide. There are perhaps 60,000 species of these parasitic wasps, and almost all of them lay their eggs in the bodies of insects or spiders. Some ichneumons listen for insect larvae moving deep inside a tree. When they find one, they drill a hole into the tree with a special egg-laying tube on their abdomen. The tube has a hard mineral coating and can penetrate solid wood. When it strikes a larva, the wasp injects its eggs into the unfortunate insect. When the eggs hatch, the young wasps eat their host from the inside out, keeping it alive just long enough for it to burrow out of the tree. Ichneumon wasps vary greatly in size, from one-eighth inch (3 millimeters) to as much as five inches (12 ½ centimeters) in length.

The **white tern** makes its home on small islands in the world's tropical seas. They have few enemies on these islands, so the terns can lay their single egg in the open. Not building a nest saves time and energy that the birds can use to search for fish and other food. The white tern often balances her egg on a forked tree branch, where it is sometimes blown off by high winds. If this happens, the mother bird quickly lays another egg. A tern chick that hatches on a tree branch must hold on with its claws until it is able to fly.

The **Polynesian megapode** is native to one small island — an active volcano — in the South Pacific Ocean. Because humans have destroyed much of the island's forest habitat, these birds are endangered, and there are only about 1,000 of them left. Their population is increasing, however, since the birds' recent introduction to a nearby island uninhabited by people. Polynesian megapodes are about 15 inches (38 centimeters) in length. They eat insects, worms, small reptiles, seeds, and fruit. Using the heat of a volcano to incubate their eggs is convenient, but it means that these birds can live only in places that are volcanically active.

Echidnas (ih-*kid*-nuhs) live in New Guinea and Australia. The only other egg-laying mammal, the platypus, is found just in Australia. Echidnas are also called spiny anteaters. They feed primarily on termites, catching them with a long, sticky tongue. Echidnas, which are about the size of a housecat, make their burrows among rocks and logs on the forest floor. Like all marsupials, they raise their young in a pouch. A newly hatched echidna, or puggle, is tiny — the size of a jellybean. It will stay in its mother's pouch until it starts to grow spines, at about eight weeks of age.

. . . use a leaf ?

The **lily trotter**, or jacana (zah-seh-*nah*), is a water bird found in most of the world's tropical regions. It can be as much as 15 inches long (38 centimeters) but weighs less than five ounces (142 grams). The bird's light weight and extra-long toes allow it to walk on lily pads and other floating leaves without sinking. As the lily trotter tiptoes across the surface of a marsh or lake, it uses its beak and claws to lift up the edges of the lily pads and looks beneath for fish and insects. These birds are good swimmers and will dive underwater to catch prey or escape danger.

The musical call of the **tailorbird** can be heard in the forests of India and Southeast Asia. Despite its loud song, the tailorbird is small — reaching only about five inches (13 centimeters) in length. A female tailorbird curls the edges of a leaf together by wrapping it with spider web silk or stringy plant material. Using its beak as a needle and the silk or plant fiber as thread, the bird sews the edges of the leaf together and forms a pouch that will hold its nest. Filled with soft grass, the nest will be snug and well camouflaged. Tailorbirds feed on insects, fruit, and nuts.

Leafcutter ants are the only animals besides humans that grow their own food. They live in the southern United States and Central and South America. A leafcutter ant nest can contain as many as 8 million insects. The ants vary in size, but most are about a half-inch (12 millimeters) long. With their sharp jaws, the ants cut the leaves of trees and shrubs into pieces. They carry them back to their nests, where other ants chop them up into even smaller pieces and lick them clean. The leaf pieces are placed in underground chambers and fertilized with the ants' waste. A small piece of fungus is placed on the mixture. With careful tending, it will grow into a crop of fungus that will feed the colony. When a new leafcutter queen leaves the nest to start her own colony, she places a piece of the fungus in a special pocket on her head. This way, the new nest will be able to grow its own food.

White tent bats are tiny, only one and a half inches (4 centimeters) long. They live in the rainforests of Central America and hunt at night, feeding on insects, fruit, and nectar. White tent bats use their sharp teeth to cut through the supporting ribs of large leaves. This causes the sides of the leaf to droop down, creating a "tent." Here the bats spend the day, hanging upside down as they sleep. Inside their tent, the bats' white fur is colored green by sunlight shining through the leaf, making it difficult for a predator to see them.

Along with gorillas, chimpanzees, and humans, the **orangutan** (aw-*rang*-oo-tan) is one of the great apes. It lives in rainforests on the islands of Borneo and Sumatra. A male orangutan can reach almost six feet (180 centimeters) in height and weigh as much as 260 pounds (118 kilograms). Females are about half this size. They spend most of their lives high in the trees, eating fruit, leaves, insects, and small animals. Orangutans often use leaves and sticks as tools. Some scientists believe that — besides humans — they are the most intelligent animals on earth. These peaceful primates are seriously endangered by hunting and the loss of their forest habitat to human farming and logging.

Capuchin monkeys (cap-*yoo*-chin) live in trees in the forests of Central and South America. They are social animals, living in groups of about a dozen animals. Capuchins grow to 20 inches (51 centimeters) in length. They eat seeds, fruit, insects, frogs, lizards, and small mammals. The most intelligent of the New World monkeys (those living in North or South America), capuchins are sometimes trained to help disabled people. Capuchins rub their bodies with the leaves of plants that are known to contain insect-repelling chemicals. Biologists also believe that the leaves may be used as a kind of perfume to make a capuchin smell good to other members of its group.

. . . catch a fly?

Jackson's chameleons come from the forests of eastern Africa. Nowadays, they are also found in Hawaii, where pet chameleons have escaped to live in the wild. These colorful lizards eat insects and worms, and are about nine inches (23 centimeters) long when full-grown. The male has three horns on its forehead, which it uses in battles with rival males. Like many other chameleon species, Jackson's chameleons can change color. Despite what many people believe, they don't do this to match the color of their surroundings. Instead, color is used as a way of communicating their emotions to other chameleons. An excited or angry chameleon may turn a series of bright hues. A frightened or worried chameleon can become almost black.

The **rainbow trout** was originally found in cold, clear streams on the Pacific coast of North America. People who fish for sport like to catch rainbows, and they have introduced this trout to many other parts of the world, including Europe, Asia, and Australia. These fish are 12 to 18 inches (30 to 46 centimeters) long. They eat insects, worms, small fish, and fish eggs.

In the dense tropical forests of southern India and Sri Lanka lives the **slender loris**, a delicate, large-eyed mammal only about eight inches (20 centimeters) in length. The slender loris spends almost all of its time in the trees. It sleeps during the day, curled into a ball with its arms wrapped around its head. At night it uses its large eyes  to catch insects and find fruit in the dim light. Slender lorises move slowly and carefully through the branches but can react very quickly to snatch an insect or avoid a snake.

The **net-casting spider** hangs upside down, holding its square web by the corners. It is waiting for an unwary insect to pass beneath. These Australian spiders are nocturnal — they hunt at night. To help them see their prey, they make a white "target" from their own droppings and position themselves directly above it. When an insect wanders over this spot, the spider thrusts out its legs, spreads its web, and pushes it down over its victim. The insect is paralyzed with a bite and wrapped in silk to be eaten at the spider's leisure. Net-casting spiders grow to be about three-quarters of an inch (2 centimeters) long.

There are thousands of species of **assassin bug,** and they are found almost everywhere on earth. Assassin bugs are very poisonous. They stalk their prey — usually other insects — or wait for it in ambush. Some assassin bugs, also called "kissing bugs," bite sleeping humans on the lips or eyelids. Their bite can cause a person's face to swell painfully. The pointed beak of the assassin bug is used as a spear, poison

injector, and drinking straw. With it the bug sucks the juices from the bodies of its victims. Assassin bugs range in size from one-eighth inch (3 millimeters) to one and a half inches (38 millimeters).

With its streamlined body and swept-back wings, the **chimney swift** is one of the most graceful flyers in the animal world. These birds spend the summer in eastern North America and fly south to Peru in large flocks every winter. Chimney swifts, so called because they often build their nests in chimneys, are about eight inches (20 centimeters) long, and spend nearly all of their time in the air. They can't stand on flat surfaces — their legs work only when they are clinging to a vertical wall or tree trunk. Chimney swifts collect the twigs used to make their nests while flying, and they drink by skimming their bill along the surface as they fly just above the water. They eat on the wing, consuming up to 40,000 flying insects a day, and even sleep in flight, gliding along with other swifts at high altitude.

. . . dig a hole?

In places along the southern coast of South America the sea is bordered by high limestone cliffs. With its powerful beak the **burrowing parrot** chisels into the soft rock of these cliffs. Working year after year, the parrots dig nest holes that may reach ten feet (3 meters) in depth. Burrowing parrots are large birds, about 20 inches (51 centimeters) in length. They leave their nests in large flocks to feed on berries, fruit, and seeds.

The **Mexican burrowing toad** is found in the southernmost tip of Texas and the arid regions of Central America. It spends much of its life underground, digging itself into the earth with its shovel-like back feet. When a heavy rain falls, male toads emerge from their burrows and call for a mate with a loud "whoa" sound. After mating, the female toad finds a puddle of water where she can lay her eggs. The puddle may dry up quickly, but the eggs hatch in two or three days, and the young tadpoles soon develop into toads. A burrowing toad can suck in air and blow its body up like a balloon. It does this to frighten predators or to push out the sides of its burrow as it digs. Mexican burrowing toads are about two and a half inches (6 centimeters) long. They feed on insects, primarily ants and termites.

Worm lizards are legless reptiles. Their eyes and ears are covered with skin, and their bodies are ringed with circular grooves, giving them the appearance of large earthworms. They spend almost their entire life underground, pushing their way through soft soil with their blunt head. Heavy rains sometimes drive worm lizards from their burrows, giving them the nickname "thunderworm." They are about 12 inches (30 centimeters) long and eat grubs, snails, and insects. Worm lizards live in warm parts of the Americas, Europe, Africa, and Asia.

The **red rock urchin** is a relative of the sand dollar and sea star. It lives in warm shallow water in the Caribbean Sea and the Gulf of Mexico. Including the sharp spines that protect it from predators, this sea urchin is about two inches (5 centimeters) across. Red rock urchins use their teeth — found on the underside of their body — to scrape away rock and coral. Eventually, they make a hole in the sea floor that becomes their home. There they feed on algae and bits of seaweed. An urchin that grows too large to get out of its burrow can survive on the food that washes into its hole.

At one time the **prairie mole cricket** was thought to be extinct. A few years ago, the insects were discovered living in a few small patches of prairie grass in the American Midwest. A male prairie mole cricket digs a Y-shaped burrow — a single tunnel with two openings. Sitting in the tunnel, he makes a loud, repetitive song by rubbing his wings together. The shape of the burrow amplifies the sound, which is intended to attract a female cricket. Prairie mole crickets are about two inches (5 centimeters) long. They feed underground, eating the roots and stems of prairie grass. Their front legs are broad and flat, specially shaped for digging in sandy soil.

Aardvarks live in central and southern Africa. They eat almost nothing but ants and termites, and they are well adapted for this diet. A sensitive nose helps them locate termite nests. Powerful front legs and long claws tear open the nests, and the aardvark sucks up thousands of insects with its long, sticky tongue. Tough skin protects it from bites, and its nostrils can be closed to keep out dirt and dust. Aardvarks are active at night, and spend the day sleeping in a system of burrows they have excavated. They are large mammals — as much seven feet (2 meters) long with their tail — but they must watch out for lions, leopards, and big snakes. Aardvarks regularly leave their burrows and dig new homes. Their old burrows provide shelter for other animals.

. . . eat a clam?

Raccoons live in forests, prairies, and marshes throughout North America. They have also become a familiar nighttime sight in many towns and cities. Raccoons are omnivores — they eat plants, fruit, insects, fish, frogs, snakes, eggs, and small birds and mammals. They have nimble fingers, and some even open doors or climb through windows to raid people's pantries and garbage pails. Raccoons average 36 inches (91 centimeters) in length and weigh about 30 pounds (13 ½ kilograms). Some people believe that raccoons like to wash their food, because they often hold it under water before they eat it. We are not certain why they do this, though it's unlikely that they are concerned with cleanliness. It may be that, like our own, a raccoon's sense of touch is improved when its fingers are wet.

The **herring gull**, along with several other species of gull, is commonly called a seagull. Herring gulls are large birds, up to 20 inches (51 centimeters) in length. They are found throughout North America but are most common along the coasts. Herring gulls are the graceful white birds often seen soaring over the beach or wading at the water's edge. They are aggressive predators, eating fish, crabs, shellfish, insects, and other birds.

There are almost 2,000 species of **sea star**, or starfish. They live in every ocean and are found in a wide variety of shapes and colors. Most have five arms, but there are sea stars with six, seven, ten, even forty arms. Sea stars appear peaceful as they lie on the ocean floor or cling to tidepool rocks, but they are fierce, slow-motion predators. The shellfish and coral they eat move slowly or not at all, so sea stars don't need to be quick. They range in size from three-quarters of an inch (2 centimeters) to three feet (91 centimeters) across. Sea stars have the ability to regrow a missing arm — some can even regrow an entire body from just one arm.

Whelks are snails found in temperate seas around the world. Their shells range in size from a fraction of an inch (a few millimeters) to two feet (61 centimeters) in length. Whelks are scavengers and predators, feeding on dead animals as well as live clams, mussels, and crabs. The whelk's mouth is located at the end of a long tube, called a proboscis. The proboscis can be much longer than the whelk's body. Holding a clam in place with its large, muscular foot, the whelk deposits a chemical that softens the clam's shell. It then bores through the weakened shell with its file-like proboscis, killing the shellfish. The whelk injects digestive juices into the clam, dissolving its body. It sucks up the liquefied clam through its proboscis and moves on, leaving an empty shell behind.

The **bat ray,** a kind of fish, lives in the eastern Pacific Ocean. A large bat ray can have a wingspan of six feet (1 ¾ meters). Like all stingrays, it has a poisonous barb on its tail, but it does not normally threaten humans. Bat rays eat fish, crabs, and shellfish. The ray hovers just above the ocean floor and flaps its wings vigorously. This fans away the mud and sand, uncovering buried clams and mussels. When the bat ray finds a clam, it crushes it with its flat, tightly packed teeth and spits out the pieces of shell.

Mantis shrimp come in two varieties: spearers and smashers. Spearers shoot a barb into their prey. Smashers, like the one in this book, use a club-shaped claw to strike attackers or victims with incredible force. The strike of a mantis shrimp is one of the fastest movements in the animal world. People sometimes call them "thumb splitters" for the damage they can do to an unwary diver's hand. Mantis shrimp are aggressive predators. They attack crabs, snails, fish, and clams, stunning them or shattering their shells with a single blow of their claw. Mantis shrimp live in warm ocean waters throughout the world, and can reach 12 inches (30 centimeters) in length.

For Jamie

— *R.P. and S.J.*

www.houghtonmifflinbooks.com

The text of this book is set in Garamond Premier Pro.
The illustrations are cut and torn paper collage.

Library of Congress Cataloging-in-Publication Control Number
2008001864
ISBN-13: 978-0-618-96634-9

Printed in Singapore
TWP 10 9 8 7 6 5 4 3 2 1

Bibliography

Attenborough, David. *The Life of Birds.* Princeton: Princeton
    University Press, 1998.
Carwardine, Mark. *Extreme Nature.* New York: HarperCollins, 2005.
Davidson, Susanna, and Mike Unwin. *The Usborne World of Animals.*
    London: Usborne Publishing, 2005.
McDonald, Rosemary, ed. *Encyclopedia of Discovery: Nature.*
    San Francisco: Fog City Press, 2002.
Uttridge, Sarah, ed. *Living in the Wild.* London: Southwater, 2002.

Today, we know more than ever before about the ocean, yet it remains a mysterious and fragile frontier that man is driven to explore (previous page).

The *Johnson-Sea Links* (right) and other submersibles have helped us to uncover more about the ocean than we learned in centuries of ocean exploration previously.

Submersibles (left) are allowing us to get closer to the ocean floor—and its remarkable inhabitants—than ever before.

Harbor Branch Oceanographic Institute

Yet these three experts admit that they've barely scratched the surface. "I wish I had more time to examine what we've already discovered," says Grassle. "But every few months, someone seems to find a fascinating new deep-sea vent community—and we just have to go investigate it."

While many scientists could easily devote their entire professional careers to hydrothermal vents, the midwater world, or El Niño alone, countless other ocean mysteries remain to be solved. Some haven't even begun to be cracked; others, though, are slowly revealing themselves to persistent researchers. Encyclopedias could be filled with recent fascinating findings, but there's only room here for a taste of their variety.

For example, WHOI scientists are now using *Alvin* to try to understand how ancient volcanic and geologic activity helped build today's earth. At Scripps Institution, one major project is seeking to pinpoint the relationship between the ocean, clouds, and our changing climate, while another searches for insights into the startling increase in the population of the great white shark off the California coast.

Constant new discoveries are changing our way of looking at the ocean and its inhabitants. Recently, for example, scientists from the Smithsonian Institution were exploring the ocean floor near the Bahamas in a *J-S-L* submersible. At a depth of more than 800 feet (250 meters), they knew they would find corals and other animals, but they weren't prepared for another sight revealed in the beam of their spotlights: an abundance of algae, small undersea plants, growing in large mats on the sea floor.

The scientists found this discovery surprising because, while animals can live quite happily in the darkness of the deep sea (as is proven by the vent communities), plants require sunlight for photosynthesis, the process through which they make their food. Yet the amount of light filtering down through ocean waters is less than a thousandth of that hitting the ocean surface. The researchers are now searching for answers to how the deep-sea algae survives on light of such little intensity—or whether it has some mysterious, unique way of feeding itself without light.

While some scientists are studying algae, others are concentrating on the ocean's most fascinating creatures: the whales and dolphins. Yet even these familiar animals are providing us with startling new information about life in the sea.

Researchers have long wondered how whales navigated their lengthy yearly migrations in the absence of landmarks. For example, humpback whales that summer off the coast of Cape Cod journey each year to the Caribbean, a trip of more than 1,000 miles (1,600 kilometers) across the open ocean. How do they do it?

Recently, a team of researchers from the California Institute of Technology and elsewhere came up with a remarkable—and convincing—answer. Whales and dolphins possess sensory organs that are extremely sensitive to the earth's magnetic field. Like magnetometers, the animals are able to chart the variations that occur in the magnetic field in different areas of the sea floor.

Apparently, migrating whales use these magnetic variations—in particular, strips of low-level magnetism that stretch from north to south along the ocean floor—to guide them. By using these "highways," the whales maintain their orientation, even in the constantly moving ocean waters.

These remarkable navigational abilities, however, may also contribute to strandings, those famous events in which large numbers of whales and dolphins beach themselves and die, often for no apparent reason. The researchers have found that most strandings occur at areas of magnetic lows that lie at the end of the migratory highways. Why the animals might be so

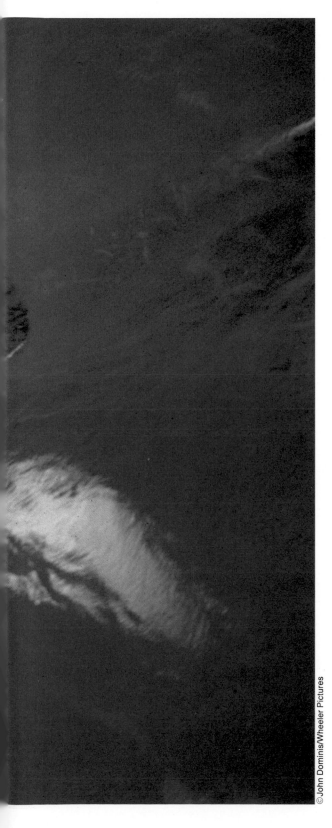

© John Dominis/Wheeler Pictures

© John Dominis/Wheeler Pictures

The strange and endangered humpback whale (above and left) is just one of countless research subjects in our ongoing attempts to understand ocean inhabitants.

W. H. O. I.

SeaPharm and other laboratories, such as this one cultivating algae beds (left) are joining the deep-sea hunt for treatments for cancer, arthritis, and a host of other diseases. They may discover remedies amid the plants and animals of the oceans (right).

determined to follow their determined paths that they would beach themselves is not yet known.

Among the most exciting current research efforts are those looking to the ocean for cures to many of our deadliest illnesses. Already, researchers have identified more than 1,500 substances, all taken from marine creatures, that have antitumor, anti-inflammatory, or other medicinal properties.

While WHOI, Scripps, and other research centers are involved in this effort, the leader in this research may be the Harbor Branch Oceanographic Institution in Fort Pierce, Florida, which has joined with SeaPharm, an international biotechnology company, in an attempt to make tomorrow's ocean our most important medical laboratory and pharmaceutical source.

The Harbor Branch/SeaPharm Project, begun in 1983, takes a meticulous approach to the search for deep-sea medicines. For example, researchers gathering a type of blue-green algae (known for its antitumor properties) first test the plant in an advanced laboratory aboard their ship. Only if the sample shows some medical promise will the investigators return to the site (either in scuba gear or aboard a *J-S-L* submersible) to harvest a larger quantity. After the plants and animals that have shown disease-fighting potential are brought back to Harbor Branch/ SeaPharm's laboratories, they are tested for potency, possible toxic side effects, and other necessary information. Those that seem particularly potent, or demonstrate unique properties, are chosen for

further purification and analysis, followed by another round of lab testing.

The most promising of these samples are then put to the most rigorous trial of all: *in vivo* testing, in which the drug—so recently found inside an algae, a sea cucumber, or some other ocean creature— is pitted against a specific disease in a human or animal patient. So far, Harbor Branch/SeaPharm has had particular success with antiviral agents, several of which are currently undergoing in vivo testing.

Not all such medical research is taking place at Harbor Branch, however. Recently, researchers at the University of California in San Diego announced a fascinating new discovery. They had been analyzing the intriguing composition of a sea whip (a type of soft coral) found in

No matter how much we learn about the ocean and its inhabitants, it will always remain our most mysterious and fascinating frontier (right).

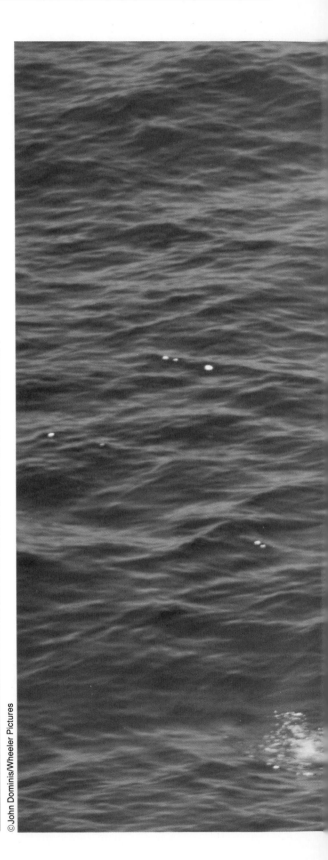

the Caribbean. What they found, however, may have exciting consequences for people afflicted with arthritis, psoriasis, and other difficult-to-treat diseases.

These sea whips, it turns out, contain compounds that seem to act as potent anti-inflammatory agents. Dubbed *pseudopterosins* by the university's William Fenical, who discovered them, these compounds seem to be up to one thousand times as potent as such currently used drugs as indomethacin. Yet they don't seem to be nearly as toxic as steroid drugs, which control inflammation but can cause terrible side effects.

The pseudopterosins are so unusual that, even after years of study, researchers don't know exactly how they work. In coming years, however, the compounds may well become a safe, effective treatment for a variety of diseases that currently plague hundreds of millions of people worldwide. They may also be just one of hundreds of such drugs

available should researchers have the opportunity to discover and extract the others now lying latent in the oceans.

Unfortunately, despite all its rich potential, the ocean environment has been under attack for many years. The problem, according to Grassle, is the same as that faced by the tropical rain forests and other of the earth's richest environments: the rate at which these areas are being thoughtlessly exploited. "The ocean is enormous, but it's also fragile," he points out. "We've already seen the consequences of overfishing—but the long-term effects of pollution may be even more severe." Yet the dumping of sewage and, recently, even the disposal of nuclear waste in the oceans continues. "We still know so little about the ocean; we haven't even begun to identify everything that's out there, much less find out what can benefit us," says Grassle. "I just hope we have enough time."

RESEARCH INSTITUTIONS AND PROGRAMS

Ametek
Straza Division
790 Greenfield Drive
El Cajon, CA 92022
(619) 442-3451

Can-Dive Services, Ltd.
1367 Crown Street
North Vancouver, British Columbia
Canada, V7J 1G4
(604) 984-9131

Harbor Branch Oceanographic Institution, Inc.
Link Port
5600 Old Dixie Highway
Fort Pierce, FL 33450
(305) 465-2400

Hydro Products
P.O. Box 2528
San Diego, CA 92112
(714) 453-2345

Ocean Drilling Program
Texas A & M University
College Station, TX 77843
(409) 845-2673

Perry Offshore, Inc.
275 West 10th Street
P.O. Box 10297
Riviera Beach, FL 33404
(305) 842-5261

Scripps Institution of Oceanography
University of California—San Diego
A-033B
La Jolla, CA 92093
(619) 534-1294

Smithsonian Institution
Washington, DC 20560
(202) 357-2627

Woods Hole Oceanographic Institution
Woods Hole, MA 02543
(617) 548-1400

I N D E X

Page numbers in italics refer to captions, diagrams, and illustrations.